HOW CAN I....

Dream Less,

Win more?

"Sound business advice and inspirational quotes to encourage teenagers and adults to become the ultimate entrepreneur"

www.howcanionline.com

First Published in Great Britain in 2009

ISBN : 978-0-9559867-0-3

'Dream less, Win More' first published in January 2009, to inspire today's generation that nothing is impossible to achieve. We all have the capabilities to becoming million pound entrepreneurs, with the right advice we can get there.

HOW CAN I....

Dream Less,

Win more?

"Sound business advice and inspirational quotes to encourage teenagers and adults to become the ultimate entrepreneur"

www.howcanionline.com

HOW CAN I...?

Content

Content

Omar Marcel Gashi

"Having ideas is all very well, putting them ideas to practice is what makes the entrepreneur"

Omar Marcel Gashi

Our Generation

Our generation of young individuals have a mind full of business ideas, which can become virtually multi million pound operating business in the future. However the problem is that many do not know where to start and many struggle to get the support that is required to start their business. It's not that the support and advice is not there, the main reason is that many individuals don't know where to get the support and advice. Because pf this the possibility of these businesses operating is thrown down the drain.

Many Youngsters believe that their age is the barrier to being successful.... is this the case? Then not too worry, you will learn through the book that you can use your age to such an extent that it becomes the factor that makes your business a success.

Become your own apprentice...become the ultimate entrepreneur!

The British Economy

The government initiative is to develop children from the early ages, from secondary school to make them more entrepreneurial minded. If we look at our economy in the mid 20th century we can outline that all products were stamped with the famous mark 'Made in Great Britain'. The UK infact used to manufacture over 50% of the worlds goods. However now the UK now only manufacturers below 7%. Which is a big drop. This is mainly due to the cheap labour costs abroad. How many of you have ended up to speaking to someone in Asia when dealing with a bill query? For Britain the future of its economy lies in the hands of the children and young adults currently in education. The Government has introduced many strategies in increasing enterprise. It has many projects which allow business minded individuals to get free support and also advice.

"The Success of the company has been based on 'teamwork' from the beginning."

Bill Gates, founder of Microsoft Corporation

The Entrepreneur

An Entrepreneur can be identified in three different ways. They all have a dream. They all have an ambition. They all want to do well. There is no age limit to an entrepreneur whether your 11 years of age in secondary school and wanting to start your own business or whether your 60 and are keen on starting your own business. This book will look at all aspects of business incorporated in real life events.

In today's society there are millions of people who relish the prospect of being their own boss and starting up their own business. In today's society anyone can achieve their full potential, with the right guidance and the right support...'nothing is impossible'.

Throughout this book there are key specifications which outline the real key on how and why people become entrepreneurs. This book will also answer many of the questions that an individual who is keen on starting their own business may want to ask.

"If you can DREAM it, you can DO it."

Walt Disney

Enterprise:

This is the term that many of you who are reading this have. Enterprise refers to the ability that is given to think of new ideas ideas and carrying them out. To be an Entrepreneur you would need to be enterprising.

Entrepreneurs are very important to the UK economy. All business have started in some way or another and all of them started very small. They are the origins of larger companies.

There are many reasons to why Individuals want to become an entrepreneur:

* To become their own boss
* The possible dream of owning a large business
* To have a second career

The list can go on and on depending on the individual. Many entrepreneurs would say that making their own decisions would be the factor which persuaded them to

start their own business, which is a true fact. As many people want to work for themselves and make decisions for themselves.

When It comes to small businesses there is no doubt that they are very vulnerable within the early stages of operating. However not many businesses know that their is free support and also advice available from the Government.

There are also other benefits available from the Government which includes Government grants. Businesses are usually offered to a business sector or pending on the geographical area that they are located. Small businesses have always played a huge role within the UK economy. In the year 2006 data was released to show that there were over 2million business operating in the UK. Thus means that 1 in 30 people own a business in the UK. Many experts within the past have stated that small business are the future for the UK.

"If it really was a no-brainer to make it on your own in business there'd be millions of no-brained, harebrained, and otherwise dubiously brained individuals quitting their day jobs and hanging out their own shingles. Nobody would be left to round out the workforce and execute the business plan."

Bill Rancic, winner on Donald Trump's "The Apprentice

"I don't have a business idea"

Well do not worry, your not alone. Many people have had similar problems we don't all think alike, thats what makes us all unique, we each have a different personality, we all have different skills, we all think differently. You as an individual might see the prospects of being involved in a business as something exciting, who can blame you? Often thats all it takes, if you are passionate and excited in running your own business the chances are you will be successful. However the excitement is very well, but now you have to look for your business idea. There are many places where to look. Usually the best business ideas are very simple. Look at your everyday life, look at any problems that you may have; see if you can have a solution to that problem. The more original the idea the better. Look at the world around you see what there is a market for, that you can cater for. If your still struggling then why not look at what already exist see if you can develop a product or a service that already exist. Make it your own, and you will have found your unique selling point (USP). An entrepreneur would usually start to look at

their own life experiences to release a potential product/service that he/she is familiar with. other forms of business ideas can come through the realisation that there is a market gap, and that gap needs to be filled.

By knowing the product/service that you want to go into, then the Entrepreneur will have a good knowledge of the products/services that they are going to be offering, which makes it a vital strength to when operating a business. Another positive factor of knowing the product/service that you will want to go into is that you will be far more likely to have a large range of contacts which you can use to your benefit, and if you have a good reputation within the market then this is also likely to help you business.

If we look at the positive factors of spotting a gap within the market and for starting a business within that market, there can be many advantages. This is most likely going to make your business much more recognisble as the business will have the 'first mover advantage'.

"Experience taught me to listen to my gut feeling"

Donald Trump - The Apprentice USA

"There is a difference between an Entrepreneur and having a good idea"

At one stage of our lives we have all had great business ideas. How many of us have done nothing with those ideas?

This is what sets the entrepreneurs apart from the normal person. To be an entrepreneur you have to make ideas happen. How many individuals have said 'if only I did this'. There is nothing that stops us from making ideas happen. Its all very well having a vision but its the factor of turning that vision into reality. In the past many people have had ideas, those ideas could have been worth millions of pounds. Your idea could be worth just as much. So make that idea happen. If you don't then you will be regretting in a later stage of life. Start your business idea, use trial and improvement, never stop until you have that business which is guaranteed to do well for you. If Sir Alan Sugar didn't make his ideas happen. Would he today have an £800 million empire? Or would he today be living in that same council house where he lived as a child?

Sugar made his idea happen now he is a millionaire, he came from a poor family and look where he is today. You have to remember when it comes to business we are all equal. We all started off somewhere, but its that somewhere where you need to start.

There is no real point of setting yourself a target that you internally know you wont achieve. How many of us say that we will do this 'tomorrow' in many cases tomorrow never comes. So keep a time management, set yourself targets on developing your idea. Don't watch the entrepreneur, be the entrepreneur. Your just as good. Its all about will power, if you can believe that you can do it, then you can do it. If you believe you cant do it, then you will not do it!

"Entrepreneurs willingly assume responsibility for the success or failure of a venture and are answerable for all its facets."

Victor Kiam, best known for his "I liked it so much, I bought the company" ads for Remington electric shavers.

Developing the Idea

When coming to develop your idea it is more than likely that you will need some source of finance. This is where many people stop their business idea because of lack of finance.

However pocket money can come in very handy. In many cases businesses have started of very small with little or no finance and some have become multi million pound operating businesses. Sir Alan Sugar the host of Apprentice who has a personal fortune of over £800 million started his business venture by saving his pocket money to invest on small business ideas. Being the 21st century the government has a variety of projects that will help with funding.

In some cases its not about funding but its about advice and also support. The best place to turn to is your school, college or university. For adults university is a great option as many would be willing to give guidance.

"I never perfected an invention that I did not think about in terms of the service it might give others... I find out what the world needs, then I proceed to invent."

Thomas Edison - Inventor

What's Stopping you?

Usually in many cases, young individuals when they have a business idea something stops them from getting close to that success. What's Stopping them? Peer pressure is the main factor which stops individuals. If this is the case then you have to look at who your peers are. Friends should support each other in all decisions made in life. If peer pressure is infact taking you away from your business idea, then you have to think to yourself which is more important; setting an image with your friends or making you business idea a reality. You have to pick and choose on what you see as most important if you are serious about your business idea and want it to progress then make it happen don't let anyone else tell you otherwise.

Peers in cases can be off putting when introducing a business idea to them. In some cases peers can also provide constructive criticism when it comes to business. So share your business idea with friends and family, get their views.

"Business opportunities are like buses, there's always another one coming."

Richard Branson founder of the Virgin Group.

Failure

Being Scared of failure is something natural that comes to the human mind. If we weren't scared of failure then there would be no real point to life. If we weren't scared of failure then it is very likely that everyone would have taken risks. In business there has to be an equilibrium between failure and success. In many cases you have to look at the percentage; if your business idea is 50.1% that its going to be successful and its 49.9% that its not going to be successful...then take the risk! Entrepreneurs are all about taking risks. That's what sets entrepreneurs out from a 'normal person'. Its often considered that the bigger the risk the higher the rewards.

Many entrepreneurs relish the prospect of taking risks as they can see a potential in that risk. However the younger you are then the more likely you should be to take risks. What have you got to loose? If one business idea fails, then you have to try another business idea until you have made your business a success. So don't be afraid of taking risks. Its natural in the business world if there were no

risks, then there would be a large amount of businesses operating. Successful individuals in the business world in one stage of their life have taken a risk which has made them successful. However as well as being willing to take risks you also have to think about failure.

"I couldn't wait for success, so I went ahead without it."

Jonathan Winters

"My age is the barrier ... I can't do it"

When it comes to age many individuals get put off especially teenagers. However not to worry. Your age is far from a barrier. In many cases it can prove helpful in developing your business.

It might feel weird at first promoting your business idea or just generally telling adults about your business. However there are many people who are in your position and who have been in your position. Young individuals are often stereotyped in the media. How many times have we heard the media speak about 'hoodies'.

However it's no all bad the media can also promote young individuals who are doing something different. Often when it comes to marketing, using the media is the simplest way of attracting business, especially if you are a teenager. Your age is not a barrier, its not a boundary, use your age to promote yourself. Many of todays entrepreneurs have started off very young.

Sir Alan Sugar started off at 11 years of age, Sir Richard Branson started off at the age of 17. There is one thing to remember its never too late to start a business. Age is not the barrier, your the barrier to yourself.

The term can't does not exist within the English dictionary. The term can does exist. But still why do people use the term can't. You need to think to yourself 'I can do it', when you often think in a positive manner then its likely that you will succeed.

The little voice inside our head is often is what puts us off from a great business venture. Your idea could be worth millions of pounds... take the risk! If you can only imagine what opening your own successful business will do for you. You will be your own boss, you will have money to spend, its whats going to set you apart from the rest.

There is no barrier to doing well, there is no barrier to aiming high, there is no barrier to opening your own business.

"Age is whatever you think it is, you are as old as you think you are."

Muhammad Ali: Boxer

Trial and Improvement

Trial and improvement is something that many entrepreneurs have experienced before. Its a process that we all go through and have been through. When babies start to walk they start using trial and improvement. They try and try and try to walk until they walk however each step that they take, they improve that one step a little bit better.

Trial and Improvement comes naturaly its not scientific. When it comes to the business world, you have to use trial and improvement when developing your business idea. In many cases this is the best way of learning. Through trial and improvement you will be able to out source any problems that your business idea may have. Trial and improvement in a business can offer many opportunities to an individual to analyse their own business. Its always considered with many individuals that the method of trial and improvement is the main way of learning not just in the business world but also in school, such as answering questions, you try once,you try twice, you try three times...until you have figured out the answer.

"Imagine"

John Lennon

Protecting Business Ideas

Business Ideas can be protected due to many reasons. An entrepreneurs view to why he/she may want to protect an idea, is that it will enable the entrepreneur to recover the cost of bringing the business idea within the market segment. Businesses protect their products, images and other material through patents, copyright and also trademarks. By protecting the business idea it will enable the entrepreneur to prevent 'copycats' entering the same market. In an investments point of view it would be wise to invest within a product that has been patented.

Copyright: This is the protection that is applied to books, plays, films and also music.

Patent: This is the exclusive right which allows the business to process or produce a product, for a fixed term usually being 20 years.

Trademark: This is a word, image, sound or a smell that enables a business to differentiate itself from others.

"Once you decide to work for yourself, you never go back to work for somebody else."

Sir Alan Sugar

Apprentice and AMSTRAD founder

Market Research

After you have looked at your business idea, then you have to look at the market that you are competing with. By looking at your competitors you will be able to look at the similarities and differences that your product/service may have with other competitors. In business there is a term given to this called "market research"

You can use two types of Market Research:

Primary Market Research: is the term given information that you find out yourself. e.g. By creating a simple questionnaire and going to the public and asking them to give feedback on your product/service. However this can prove to be very costly and therefore is suited to established companies.

Secondary Market Research: is the cheapest form of Market Research. It involves using the information that has already been provided and by using the context of your research to your business. e.g if a company wanted

to know how many people wash their cars in the summer period then the company can use secondary research by getting details from the local car wash outlet .

When conducting market research you will be soon to find your Unique Selling Point (USP) of the company. The USP is a term that refers to what makes your company different from any other. If you want to be successful the recipe to success is your USP. If its different than something that already exists then your product/service is much more likely to stand out.

Its almost the feeling you get when you go to a magazine shop...what catches your attention?; Often its the magazine that stands out from the rest. Now imagine that your business is one of those magazines ... what does your business have to do? The obvious answer is to stand out. So when you are thinking of your business idea make it original, make it stand out!

"I want to do it because I want to do it."

Amelia Earhart

"You only live once, if you don't enjoy it, it's your fault, nobody else's."

Duncan Banatyne - Part of the Dragons on the BBC and self- made millionaire.

The Business Plan:

The business plan is a very important aspect when it comes to business enterprise. The business plan is the document that is designed to allow a business make predictions for its operations for the future. It makes key decisions and also can prepare you for problems and opportunities that can arise with your business. Its very important especially if you are a start-up businesses. If you are applying for a grant or loan or any form of funding then the first document that will be asked from parties will be the business plan.

The Business Plan is the first impression that a potential investor of your business will see so it need to be up to scratch. They can range in size with a small company having a business plan of 3 pages to a large international company having a business plan of 3000 pages. However what you have to remember is in many cases its not the quantity but its the quality and the input that is put in the plan. What makes an effective Business Plan is that it has to portrait a clear message that the business is going to

be successful...or else there will be little investment.

There are a number of purposes of a business plan. The first main reason is that it really makes the entrepreneur think about their business. If you are making a business plan you have to know your business. In many cases individuals who cannot complete their business plan usually end up not surviving in its first year. The business plan can also prove to be a problem solver which will help save time and also money as it will have a main course of action if a problem arises.

The business plan as stated earlier allows the entrepreneur to apply for funding if needed. If its through banks, investors or any other party will want you to present your business plan.

Many entrepreneurs fall short after the business plan stage as they do not update their business plan. However the good entrepreneur will update their business plan as often as it should be updated as it is an essential planning tool. It provides regular checks on the progress of the

business and also includes cash flow forecasts, objectives etc...

The contents of the Business Plan :

Many individuals believe that business plans should all look alike however this is not the case. A business plan should be designed in its unique way depending on the business type, size and also service/product it offers. The business plan should also be made personal aswell by adding content from yourself e.g your personal goals and also key elements that you believe will make your business a success.

The Executive Summary :

This is just an overall descriptions of the main features of the business. This is usually the most important factor within the business plan. Its usually the only part that many individuals will read on your business plan. It should be kept basic with an overall view of the rest of the sections that are included within the business plan.

Business Description:

This is the term that is given to the description of the history of the business and also its start up plans, the structure that the business has and also it would include the following :

* The length of time that the business has been running
* The sector that the business is located in
* The Structure of the business (Sole Trader, Partnership, Limited etc...)
* The business objectives for future long term goals

Analyising the Market:

This term refers to analyising the market and also the competitor that your business has. It would also include information about your customers (who are they? where are they? etc...)

The section should include the following:

* The market
* The customer
* The competition
* The future of the market

Strategy and Implementation:

This term refers to the analysis of the decisions that need to be carried out within the business. Also you will have to state who will be carrying out this role, this should include information on :

* Pricing
* Promotion
* Sales Strategies

Production and strategies could include :

* Location (isit owned or rented)
* Production (are they owned or leased)
* Systems (stock control, quality control)

Financial Plan

This will include key financial documents that are required such as profit or loss margins, cash flow forecast and also a balance sheet. It should also include key financial rations aswell as any other assumptions or financial objectives.

What it takes to create the business plan:

Planning: This is a key skill that is required in itself and its the ability to plan and be organised at the same time.

Numbers: An entrepreneur cannot be afraid to use numbers, financial information is important within a business plan.

Vision: The entrepreneur needs a clear idea of the business and its Unique Selling Point (USP)

Determination: An entrepreneur needs to be determined to complete the plan as accurately as possible.

"Stand out from the rest"

The legal structure of the business:

The structure of the business is the decision that is usually taken on after you have decided of what business you are going to operate. This is an important part of your business as it can affect the following :

* How much tax and NI the business will pay
* The way decisions are made
* The sources of finance that are available
* Records and also accounts that will be required to keep

The Limited Company:

Offers Limited Liability to its owners. What this means is that if the company ever goes into debt then the owners cant be held liable for the company. Imagine the Limited company as a virtual employee the company pays you. Therefore if the company does go into liquidation owing money then you cannot be held liable. Therefore this does mean that your possessions such as your home or car

etc... will not be affected to loss. There is often a lot of paperwork involved with a Limited company and its always worth getting a solicitor .

Sole Trader

The Sole trader has Liability on the business which means you are the company. This does mean that you will be liable for any debt. If your business was ever at risk and was owing money then you would be risking your home, car etc... On the other hand there are positive factors to being a Sole Trader;It will allow individuals to keep 100% of the profit.

Partnership

A partnership is a business that shares its liability between 2 -20 individuals, thus means if you were keen on opening a business with your friends, family etc... then the partnership would be best suited to you. The liability is shared.

"Can you see yourself here...yes? Don't dream it... be part of it"

Finance:

Internal Source of Finance:

This is the finance that comes from the business owner or its shareholders. This could include personal funds, or profit made through the business.

Personal sources of finance:

The owner of a small business start-up will usually have had to put money within the business. The money would have been the owners personal money. However in some cases it can be money that has been borrowed from friends or family.

There are some major advantages of obtaining finance internally:
* There usually would be no restrictions in the use of the money
* Its a sign of confidence as the entrepreneur is putting money within a business

* When borrowing from friends or family means that rarely there is interest to be paid
* Family and friends would be willing to lend money

External sources of finance

This refers to the finance that is obtained outside from the business. Which can include bank loans, overdrafts and also venture capital.

Overdraft

This is the most flexible source of finance, it can be very useful when there is a little money coming in to the business. Banks usually charge a fee on issuing an overdraft and also have interest placed on the overdraft which can be very high. Therefore its not a good source of finance if it was needed to be used for a long term use.

Other external sources of finance include bank loans and also share capitals.

"Your business idea could potentially be worth millions"

Locating the Business:

The location of the business can prove to be a huge marketing tool depending on what business you wish to operate. In many cases the most important factor of business is to be located close to the customers. If you wish to operate a retail outlet the location needs to be perfect. This is due to the reason that your business has to be placed where the customer expects you to be.

Heavy footfall areas such as the town center can influence new customers to enter your premises. You will also need to consider the location of the competitors. You may wish to be close to them or the opposite. However in many cases it would be beneficial to be placed near a competitor so customers have a choice in visiting alternatives.

Because of IT it has become less important for the physical location of the business. Business are located in less traditional places such as warehouses and small offices in order to save money but however they are still

reaching their customers through the Internet.

In some cases some entrepreneurs go into business in order to work from home as its a key decision to why opening up their own business. Therefore the location is not a real issue.

There is no doubt that location can affect businesses, this is why many businesses operate from home. The main reason being that the Internet has the ability for entrepreneurs to work from home. This can be referred to as teleworking. There are a number of benefits from working at home but there are also some drawbacks from running a business at home. Advantages include reduced costs as there will be no costs being paid for the premises. There is also no lengthy lease agreements and lastly allows entrepreneurs to get quick advice from friends an family.

"Success is there if you know its there"

**Michael Bloomberg - New York Mayor &
millionaire.**

Marketing

Marketing is the main part of a business. So you have a business idea but who knows about it? There is no real point of having a business if potential customers don't know that you exist. This is where Marketing comes in. In many cases many companies spend millions of pounds on marketing costs its a way of making yourself heard. The bigger companies such as British Airways market any flight deals they have through many different forms of marketing. Marketing can come in a variety of forms:

TV Advertising: This is the most popular way of advertising for bigger companies although it can prove to be very effective, its very costly. Radio Advertising: Radio advertising is one of the main ways that the local companies market their products; through local radio stations. Usually the cost is fairly cheap which target a diverse range of potential customers.

Newspaper Advertising: National newspaper advertising can prove to be very costly however again it can increase your potential business revenue dramatically. If your planning on setting up your own business at a local base then local newspaper advertising might be another option.

Usually the costs of advertising on a local newspaper are reasonably low and they can create a high interest on your business. All these forms of marketing are available to promote your business. However they all involve spending money. Not to worry. Many businesses have gone into the social networking sites such as Facebook and Myspace to promote themselves and many have seen a dramatic rise in sales and it's free!

"Dreams will stay dreams, unless you use your dreams to make something happen"

Omar Marcel Gashi

"Whatever you fear most has no power.. it is your fear that has the power."

Oprah Winfrey - Presenter

Employees:

Full-time employees:

In an entrepreneurs point of view employing full time staff can be beneficial to the business. The benefits include :

* Employees can build a relationship with employee
* Employees are available in emergencies
* You will create a sense of trust with them
* Higher output will be possible as they will be putting more hours within work

As with everything there are drawbacks:

* There will be high costs created by employing individuals full-time
* The employees could find it harder to improve their skills

Part -Time Employees:

Benefits include :

* There is flexibility within the hours worked
* Can be used when there are busy stages of the business
* Can be a starting point for a start-up business
* Part-time staff share skills

The disadvantages of Part-time employees:

* May find it hard to access training opportunities
* May be harder to communicate with part-time employees
* Less likely to build relationships with customers

There are many ways of employing individuals. If you are looking to recruit students then the most popular way of advertising your vacancy is by using GumTree (www.gumtree.co.uk) here you will be able to post your latest job vacancies and the website is a favorite among

many students. If you are looking to recruit experienced staff then your local paper would be your best option usually its not that expensive and job posts will include a mention on the newspapers website aswell.

Sales Personnel :

Sales personnel are a huge addition to any company. From high street chains to online businesses. They are employed for a variety of reasons. The main and obvious reason is to increase sales within the business. They generate a larger revenue as more sales are carried out. They can also cross-sell which means that they can link to products and they can sell both of them.

A good example is that a sales personnel may sell you a Play Station 3 console and then they will link that with the games for the Play Station 3 you will be far more likely to purchase a game aswell as the console. They may also be required to upsell which means for potential customers they may decide to sell exclusive items. A good example of this is that if you go into a TV shop and you look at a

normal resolution TV then the sales personnel may introduce you to a HD TV as an exclusive purchase.

Personal Selling can have many benefits to businesses:

* Likely to increase sales turnover.

* The employees will be motivated to work harder

* The sales personnel will be able to give customers professional advice.

Not everyone can become a good sales person studies have shown. However research has shown that if you have a passion for something and you want to do well then the likely chance is that you will succeed and do well.

Sales people need to have a good knowledge of the product that they are selling. This is because customers tend to ask questions and the questions need to be

answered thoroughly and this is why sales people should have sound product knowledge. You need to be able to know your product in order to sell it. You also need to be motivated to sell. It's those who enjoy the job who usually come out on top. Therefore if you feel you don't enjoy it then it could be worth considering employing staff who get a 'buzz' when selling. You also need to keep up to date with product knowledge especially if its in the technology field. You should know about the latest products and also products that will be coming to your business within the future in order to stay ahead of the game. Good sales people also know not to lie to their potential customers. Therefore you need to be as honest as possible to when selling your product.

In order to keep increasing sales you need to motivate staff to do better. Sales people who are rewarded are for more likely to be enthusiastic about the product that they are trying to sell.

Commission and Bonuses: This is a great way of rewarding and motivating sales staff; the more they sell

the higher the bonuses and commission.

Sales Incentives: This is the term which refers to rewards such as vouchers, product vouchers etc... the rewards are only given to staff who preform well.

Law affecting personnal selling:

When you buy a product / service then you automatically enter a sales contract. This is the same as a written contract. If you offer to purchase an item and the seller accepts your offer then the contract has been made.

The contract can be ended in 3 different ways:

* You accept the product and you pay for it
* You return the product
* The buyer has supplied faulty items

"Only buy something that you'd be perfectly happy to hold if the market shut down for 10 years."

Warren Buffett founder of Berkshire Hathaway, He is the worlds richest person valued at $62 Billion as of 2008.

Stand Out

When you are selling you have to make yourself different from your competitors, this can be done in many ways:

* Set an image, if your a retail outlet set a distinctive image that sets you apart from other businesses, change your shop front, the colour of the shop, the design and also layout.

* Offer Special facilities if you have the money e.g toilets, cafe etc...

* Choose to open longer hours

* If possible operate online and on the high street.

* Have sales promotions or reduce you prices in order to catch the attention of potential customers.

"Always think outside the box and embrace opportunities that appear, wherever they might be"

Lakshmi Mittal - Worlds 4th wealthiest individual as of 2008. **Founder of Mittal Steel**.

First Impressions matter:

Greet your customer in a friendly manner, try to feel confident and develop a relationship with the customer, don't try and be too demanding. When you provide information try to know about the product, you also need to have a good vocabulary. When it comes to asking questions do so but in a sensitive manner so the customer does not feel forced to buy a product, use open and closed questions depending on the customer.

Try and phrase your questions in a tactical manner. However its all very well asking questions you must listen to the customers answers and work with the answers by linking the question with the answer.

Your body language should be smooth. Give the customer space if they feel forced in any way, shape or form then it is very likely that they will leave with no purchase.

Identify customer benefits:

Identifying specific customer benefits allows you to focus on major key selling points:

* Value for money

* Reliability , this refers to the products reputation

* Complementary products this refers to the extended range of the product e.g laptop accessories

* Convenience and accessibility because its available through a variety of forms e.g locally or online

" *I've learned that mistakes can often be as good a teacher as success.*"

Jack Welch - Former chairman of General Electric

Online business:

In 2006 it was stated that there were over 76 million websites worldwide with over 6 billion pages of extended information. Websites can range in many forms from information websites to business websites, from charity websites to government websites, the list is endless...

In 2006 over £26billion was spent online in the UK alone and figures are increasing over 20% each consecutive year. With faster broadband and a wide variety of products available online there is no doubt that the future lies with the Internet.

There are many business online activities which include:

* Information : BBC, The Sun, Street Finder etc...

* Internet services : Google, Yahoo, Hotmail

* Direct selling of goods : Ebay, Amazon, Argos

" Nobody can think straight who does not work.
Idleness warps the mind."

Henry Ford - Founder of the Ford Motor Group

Direct Selling of Goods:

This is the term that is given to websites where you can shop online. Many high street stores have now also gone online which enable customers to purchase online which is a quicker and easier method of obtaining products. By buying items in bulk the stores can sell them far more cheaply online which is a huge advantage. If you are thinking of operating online you need to think about geographical issues. Your products will be available worldwide? therefore you need to think about who you want to sell to, whether you want to sell national or internationally. Also you need to take into account P&P charges.

You also will need to think about online transactions if you will be operating online. Can the customer purchase from you online? One of the features of the website must include an ordering system and the facility for processing payments securely. A favorite with many businesses is Pay-pal this is a secure method that businesses incorporate into their website and it can be a vital tool to

have in order to increase turnover. If you have a website but do not have the system installed. Then not to worry you can go to the Pay-Pal website (www.paypal.co.uk) and embed the code to your website.

If you are short on money and you need to promote your business online then the best option would be to use Interactive customization. This is the term that refers to websites that are intelligent where they can be adapted through the users preference. A good example of this is Myspace. Where you can create your own website in minutes free of charge with no HTML knowledge needed. Here you can add the Pay-Pal feature free of charge which will promote your business website within minutes. However if you are not to keen on using Myspace then your next option would be to use Ebay. Ebay allows users to offer goods for sale and the pay pal system is already installed. This is a trusted website where many full time businesses run, some are making over £70,000 a month.

www.myspace.co.uk
www.ebay.co.uk

Creating the Website:

If you are thinking of going online you need to create a website. You need to think about whether to create the website in-house or whether to ask a professional company create it.

In-house: This is the term that refers to where a basic website can be created using 'off -the -shelf' products. These are available to purchase from large Technology outlets. Where a wizard enables non professionals to create their basic website. Information on setting up a website can be accessed by contacting one of the agencies on our 'Business Help Pages' at the back of this book. You will require sufficient knowledge and also skills if you want to use packages such as Dreamweaver and Flash technology.

Outsource:

Many business however choose on to employ professionals to create a web-site. A web-design agency

can prove an important factor if you want to sell products online. The cost of employing a web-site agency can range from £2000 - £100,000.

Skills that are needed to operate an online business:

* Technical skills will be needed so the site stays online and is secure

* Maintenance skills are also needed in order to update the website

* Admin and Customer service skills are needed to respond to queries

* Management Skills are also needed which will take on account the legal responsibilities related to operating online, and also to identifying future opportunities.

When it comes to operating online you have to plan effectively. You have to choose a suitable domain name.

**Remember your domain name should
reflect your business**.

The benefits of an online business:

Benefits of going online can vary this is because you need to take into account the size of the business and also the business activity that is going to be carried out online. Many businesses go online to increase turnover or to make themselves known at a national and international scale.

Market presence: The benefits of online trading

Global Presence: The website will be available to customers on a worldwide basis. This will increase the companies trading opportunities and also market the business.

24 **hour presence**: The website will be available 24 hours a day, 7 day a week , 365 days a year and this allows the time difference not to be an issue as orders can be taken in from any time of the day.

" The world is changing very fast. Big will not beat small anymore. It will be the fast beating the slow."

Ruport Murdoch : **Media Mogul**

Finding the right balance

If your in Primary school, Secondary School, College or even University, having got your business idea you have to consider that no business is guaranteed that it will be 100% successful if it was then everyone would be involved with business. As stated earlier its the risk factor that makes entrepreneurs who they are! In many cases many entrepreneurs have had a business while still in school, however still they have come out on top with their grades and achievements. Its great to have a business idea however if you have little general knowledge of how business works, if you are more interested in "splashing" the cash rather than focusing on your studies, then STOP!.

Education is one of the most important factors in a humans life. What you learn is something that will stay with you for the rest of your life. However money comes and goes whereas knowledge is always with you. Its what makes an individual. What you learn in education will be vital when operating a business , you will be coming to the real world...What is the real world? The real world is where there will be no teacher to spoon feed you to do

something right. Infact in the "real world" there will be millions of people just like you, you will be competing with them... you have to out shine.

Your Educational background has got to be there to help you outshine in the Business world. You will be fighting to get a client/customer you have to use your initiative to make your dreams happen. No one can do that for you.

"Team work is essential in business"

Focus: Duncan Banatyne

Of course Duncan Bannatyne is the famous figure in the almighty Dragons Den. He founded Bannatynes Leisure. He was born in Glasgow, and was raised in a council house in the Clydebank area of the city, he was one of seven kids where he shared his bedroom with three of his brothers. Like many of today's entrepreneurs Bannatyne left school at an early age of 15 with no real formal qualification.

He went on to the navy where he served at the Ark Royal. Bannatyne up to the age of 30 was trying different jobs however none were for him. At the age of 30 he decided to buy an ice-cream van for £450. After investing his profits on further ice-cream vans Bannatyne was the

owner of 6 vans generating him an income of £70,000 per annum. After this Bannatyne believed that the rewards could be higher in property so he sold the business.

He then started purchasing terraced council homes where he would offer shelter for the unemployed in return the government would give him a substantial sum of money.

However its not until Bannatyne saw a local report where the government was stated that there was a shortage of nursing homes and the government would be prepared to subsidies patients for around £260 per person each week. Seeing this opportunity Bannatyne invested into land and built his own nursing home in 1986. The demand for the nursing home was very high and the business was valued at £650,000 which allowed Bannatyne to re-mortgage and to pay off all his debts.

After this Bannatynes next step was to build an 18-bedroom extension and he went on to buy land to to build a second home. After borrowing £6million he had an empire chain of around 30 homes. He floated the company

Quality Care Homes on the stock market, which paid off all his debts and he made a £1million profit for himself. At this time he had 73% stake in the public limited company, but then he went on to sell this to make £26 million.

The main reason of this was due to the reason that he stated he had to keep the city inspectors happy instead of running the business on how he wanted it to be run. He then focused on the Just Learning Nursery School brand further.He then opened his own gym after figuring out that his local gym was miles away. At this stage currently Bannatynes personal fortune is worth over £200 million.

Focus : Sir Alan Sugar

Alan Sugar, is the host of BBC's programme The Apprentice he has a personal fortune worth around £800million. However not many people know that he started on a Hackney Council estate. He was the fourth child of a poor family, and like Bannatyne he worked his way up the social ladder and work his way to the top.

His first business was at the age of 11 where his enterprise involved taking pictures of children in his school and then selling these pictures to the children loved ones. Other enterprises that he had was that he made and sold ginger beer, he also cleaned cars and also sold repackaged camera film. By the time that he had left school he was

earning more than his father.

Sugar's first realistic money making business was selling car aerials to vehicle accessory shops. At the age of 21 Sugar had founded AMSTRAD (standing for Alan Michael Sugar Trading).

At the age of 33 he floated the business on the London Stock Market where his business was valued at over £1.2 billion. His success was mainly due to the reason that he spotted a successful product so the like of Hi-fis, video recorders, computers etc... he then copied these products and made them selling them cheaper than the market leader. This is called the 'me too' method. However, because of competition from firms using Chinese labour and components Sugars profit margins fell.

Sugar was asked about his failures his response is very optimistic 'Apple have been in the pits, nearly bankrupt and then suddenly the iPod pulls them out of trouble' Back in 2007, Sugar sold AMSTRAD to BskyB in a £125m.

"Innovation distinguishes between a leader and a follower"

Steve Jobs: Major Force behind Apples success

Focus: Peter Jones

Peter Jones was born in 1966 and was raised in Berkshire. When he was seven Peter Jones would often go to his father's work place where he "loved sitting in his big chair and pretending to be in charge of a big company". His parents sent him to a private school for a couple of terms because they believed that this was the best option.

Peter Jones stated that it was "financially crippling" for them to send him there. At the age of eight he left the private school and went back to a state school which is where he spent his school years. His parent worked for over 50years to provide for the family with what they could. Peter Jones however always wanted more and he knew that "one day I was going to be a multi millionaire".

"I remember sitting for hours in my father's office leather chair, dreaming of running a multi-million pound business"

This was a big dream for a school boy however it was a dream that came true. At the age of 16 he already had a good sense of figures. After completing his Lawn Tennis Association's coaching exams, he then went on to open his own tennis coaching school at the age of 16. This allowed him to combine his two two main favorite subjects Sports and Economics.

During the age of 20, Peter was running a computer business that allowed him to own "a nice house, a BMW, a Porsche, and plenty of money to spend". However through personal mistakes Peter lost the business the hard way. So it was back to stage one, He started a computer support business, which then led him to opening a restaurant. He lost these two businesses.

At the age of 28 he decided to join a corporate business, because he was "broke without a car or a house". Within 12 months, he ended up running the business in the UK.

After these costly mistakes Peter Jones founded Phones International Group in 1998, the business was providing mobile cellular solutions to a range of client. At the moment the business operates under the brand name Data Select. The company in its first year of sales accounted for £14million of Sales. By the end of the second year sales had risen to over £44 million.

Companies that started from Phones International have been sold for millions. Generation Telecoms was sold within two years of operating to a leading mobile phone provider for millions of pounds.

Phones International Group works with every leading mobile phones provider. The groups turnover is Estimated to be worth over £150 million mark. However his business investments are not just on a telecommunications after

joining the BBC 2's Dragons Den Peter Jones has invested in Wonderland Magazine, a new luxury lifestyle magazine, The Generating Company, a contemporary circus company, i-Teddy and Reggae Reggae Sauce just to name a few.

Peter Jones has also worked with the likes of Simon Cowell to produce the hit American TV series for ABC : The American Inventor. Which will be broadcasting in Virgin 1 in the UK soon. In April 2006 Peter Jones also signed a deal with ITV to produce and start in the business show Tycoon which was aired in the summer period in 2007. Where he added further investments to his portfolio which have included , Be-Eco, Hair Rehab and the winner Bladez Toyz.

In 2008 The Sun Newspaper asked Peter Jones to sit an A level examination in business. With nothing to lose apart from dignity Peter Jones accepted the challenge. His mark at the end of the exam which is took by students in college was an A. Quite a life wouldn't you say so?

"We're all working together; that's the secret."

Sam Walton founder of the US store Wal-Mart

Focus : **Richard Branson**

Sir Richard Branson was raised in a traditional family and studies at Stowe School, where he first put his entrepreneurial mind into work where he released a national magazine entitled Student when he was just 16 years of age. At the age of 17 he went on to open a Student Advisory Center, which aimed at helping young individuals. At the age of 20 Sir Richard Branson founded the brand Virgin, as a mail order record retailer, after a little while he opened his own shop in Oxford Street in London.

In the year 1972 he built a recording studio in Oxfordshire where he signed his first artist Mike Oldfield, recorded "Tubular Bells, which was released in 1973. The first album of Virgin Records sold more than five million copies. At the age of 27 Sir Richard Branson signed the Sex Pistols to the record label after very other label in the Great Britain

turned the group down. Over the year the record label signed many top named artists which have included, Steve Winwood, Paula Abdul, Belinda Carlisle, Genesis, Phil Collins, Peter Gabriel, Simple Minds, The Human League, Bryan Ferry, Culture Club, Janet Jackson, and The Rolling Stones.

Branson managed to turn the Virgin Music Group into a giant success. In the year 1992 the Virgin Music Group was sold to Thorn EMI in a $1 billion deal. The Virgin group have however expanded to "Megastore", music retailing, books and also publishing. Also Clubs and also hotels throughout 100 companies in a combination of 15 countries.

The Virgin Atlantic Airways started in 1984, it operates a large number of Boeing 747 aircraft's to many destinations. Which have included New York, Los Angeles, Washington, Tokyo and many more... The air line has won many awards in the Past in won "Airline of the Year Award" in 2004 for three consecutive years. In the year 1993 the Virgin Group Companies had a combination of sales over $1 billion US. Aswell as being involved in businesses Branson is also involved with many charities which include

the Healthcare Foundation a leading charity which enforces health education campaign.

Sir Richard Branson lives in London and Oxfordshire he is married with two children.

"People first, then money, then things"

Suze Orman : Host of the Suze Orman Show

Omar Marcel Gashi

It first started when I was 13. I used to get pocket money but that was not enough I always wanted to stand apart from the rest. I've always wanted to do something different. It was at 13 when I was thinking to myself I have got to do something, I used to love football infact I still do but I figured that I was never going to become one.

It was the summer term and I was listening to a radio station called Takeover Radio which is the only radio station in the UK and In Europe that is presented by children. I thought to myself what do these children on this radio have that I don't... so I decided to research on the radio station if they had any opportunities to become a Radio Presenter. I was on the Internet when I came across something on the BBC website about Takeover Radio "Could you be the next radio star" That automatically drew me in, curiosity made me click on that link the link which would make me involved with Takeover Radio. After looking at BBC's article I found out that Takeover needed a radio presenter so within a matter of

minutes I decided to give the radio station a ring. After being invited to look around the radio station I was drawn in to it and I wanted to be part of it.

"Look at all your options, consider all that can go wrong and right"

Susanne Klatten - BMW and Atlana

I remember the day clearly when I joined it was Mothers Day, that Sunday all the presenters had their day off and the management of the station had their day off. However I didn't want to let this chance go to waste. I had to join that Sunday, I was invited to a 10 week training session. Where I met others in my position all wanting that radio show. It was called an audition as we were doing the training we were also being auditioned at the same time. We had various forms of checks, we had a voice test to see who had the strongest addictive voice for radio. We also looked at all aspects of radio programming, such as interviews, open and closed questions, how to keep the listener entertained etc... all of this was done at the age of 13.

After the auditions I progressed to an intensive examination period. In order to get the show we had to excel in all aspects of the training. After passing the exam and the auditions, I was "Next Generation Show" .This show was a prototype show that was aired to 103.2fm with a possible target audience of 270,000. After management were happy with my performance I then went on to get my own radio show.

"The men who have succeeded are men who have chosen one line and stuck to it."

Andrew Carnegie : Steel Business.

I presented my first show with Anick Soni called 'Dance Style UK'. One message which I will never forget at my time in radio was a message from some visitors who were coming to Leicester from Durham to see their new grandson "*I love your show you guys are doing a wonderful job what a shame we cant pick up this radio station in Durham were coming to Leicester to see our new Grandson we love your show keep up the good work*" To get that message at the age of 13 was great, there's a feeling that you get when you get something like that words can not describe. To have someone who is far older that you and to be listening to you on the radio and enjoying your show, to me its a feeling that I will never forget. However the messages on the show were coming in rapidly we were always so busy and thats when my love for radio started, it wasn't me who was listening to the presenter now I was the presenter!

When people tell me that yeah "I have a business idea however I haven't got enough time to make anything happen."I don't believe them. We all have time, its the reason that we don't want time that we don't make things

happen. In December 2006 I was put on the "Drive Time Show" a radio show that had the peak listeners of the radio station. At the age of 15 I was presenting to all individuals. Parents picking their children from school, I was presenting to individuals at the office I was presenting to a wide audience. I would go to school at 8am and I would finish at 2:50pm. My radio show would start at 3:00pm. I commuted every weekday to the city center to present a 3 hour show.

"Successful businesses start off at a small scale"

Omar Marcel Gashi

With no producer, presenting the show was even harder, I had to use my own initiative from the latest gossip stories to holding a competition draw I had to do this while presenting the show where other radio stations employ up to 3 individuals to do the jobs. Often what I did enjoy at the job was meeting a variety of different people. I had one listener who had followed me each step that I had made and asked me for my autograph which was something that brought a smile to my face. However since then I have had many people say I want your autograph and often in schools and colleges I've had individuals say "oh my god your the guy off the radio", I've also has the pleasure of meeting many celebrities the likes of "Booty Luv, The Pussycat Dolls, Blue" just to name a few.... again this made me determined to stay into radio and broaden my horizons in the media world. When people would ask me I cant believe your doing this what do you get from it... What I have always said was that its something that I can add onto my experience its a learning curve.

I was presenting to Parents picking their children from school, I was presenting to individuals at the office, I was

presenting to a wide audience. I would go to school at 8am and I would finish at 2:50pm. My radio show would start at 3:00pm. I commuted every weekday to the city center to present a 3 hour show. With no producer, presenting the show was even harder, I had to use my own initiative from the latest gossip stories to holding a competition draw I had to do this while presenting the show where other radio stations employ up to 3 individuals to do the jobs. Often what I did enjoy at the job was meeting a variety of different people. I had one listener who had followed me each step that I had made and asked me for my autograph which was something that brought a smile to my face.

Since then I have had many people say I want your autograph and often in schools and colleges I've had individuals say "oh my god your the guy off the radio", I've also has the pleasure of meeting many celebrities the likes of "Booty Luv, The Pussycat Dolls, Blue" just to name a few.... again this made me determined to stay into radio and broaden my horizons in the media world.

"Being an entrepreneur can enable you to meet a large variety of new people"

Friends often used to say "you live at your radio" however they did have a point I didn't have time for friends nor family. My life revolved around radio. After 6pm...after my show I then had to go home being the 2 main last years of Secondary school I had big GCSE's exams coming up and I couldn't fail the exams I wanted to do well in education but also out of education; I wanted to broaden my experience. When it came down to it I found the right equilibrium to spending time with friends, to working, to getting good GCSE results. So if you think you haven't got enough time to start your business then think again.

At the age of 16 still in secondary school, still presenting at radio. I decided to join a local newspaper called Re-Load this magazine was handed out around Leicestershire schools 30,000 copies were printed. My first article was entitled "Money makes the world go around" The response that I got for the article was amazing, I often have had people ask me when am I going to write again for the magazine. At the age of 16 I also set my self a goal. To become self-employed. I wanted to start my own business by the time I started college. The business is

called 'How Can I' under the Solution Media group. The business offers many opportunities for individuals, one of our main key business factors is that we offer businesses the chance to get advice on beating the credit crunch from economic specialists. Its never too late to start your own business, I started off as being that 13 year old boy who was sitting around at home on a summers day listening to the radio. We all have a starting point, you have to find where your starting point is.

"You don't need to have a 100-person company to develop that idea."

Larry Page : Founder of Google Inc.

Q&A

How did you get individuals to take you seriously?

First of all to get people to take you seriously you have to have self confidence then people will take you seriously. In todays world many of the youngsters have great ideas however its the fear factor that lets you down. I personally found it very hard to get people to take me seriously. However you have to keep on going until theres that someone who does take you seriously. Look at your business, believe in what you do.

It took me several months until I had someone agreeing to help me with my business for you its going to be much easier. There is a list of contacts that can help you with your businesses from support to finance. Your not alone if you believe in your product there is a high chance people will take your seriously. However if you lack passion on a product then you are almost guaranteed to fail. The decision that you make could be life changing? Make the right decision believe in what you do!

"Our business is about technology, yes. But it's also about operations and customer relationships."

Michael Dell - Founder of Dell Computers, Self made billionaire.

How did you develop your skills to become the entrepreneur you are today?

In school I had always been that person who spoke a lot but also the person who always put his hand up giving the right or wrong answer. I had self confidence from an early age. I felt that throughout my school age I had always wanted to something different than everyone else. I became involved In many projects in school and outside school. I love meeting new people so I tried to meet as many new faces as possible again this increased my self-confidence. The skills came through interaction with friends, family , teachers. The reason to why I believe that school is so important is that this is where I believe the most important factor of the human phase begins. In school you can develop your skills, the skills that you develop in school will be needed in the 'Real World.'

Finance... How did you access it?

My business howcanionline.com didn't need any finance because through friends who were good at graphic design

in school, I would by them a muffin and they would develop a logo which would be worth £400.

I also needed a website for my business, for the type of website that I required I was given a quote of £16,000. I didn't have that kind of money. Again I used my own initiative I advertised for online for free, asking for "University Volunteer: Website Designers" Through that I was able to cut costs expenditure by 99%. However there are government schemes that allow you to get access to finance a full contact list is available at the back pages of this booklet.

How did you overcome any obstacles that you faced?

I faced many obstacles one of the obstacles was that I had no knowledge of a business plan. Therefore I attended a training event at Business Link Leicester hire where I was able to create a business plan but also I was able to make new contacts and get advice from business professionals.

Another problem that I had was that I had no idea of how to market my product within such a large industry and I had to find out what my unique selling point was. So I attended another training event, after learning the key factors of marketing, I met individuals who were at the start up stage of their business, we related to each- other and we still keep on regular touch if we ever have a problem we call eachother and get advice. However its all about trial and improvement.

"There is an immutable conflict at work in life and in business"

Philip Knight - Founder of Nike

Where do you see yourself in 5 years time?

In 5 years time I hope to have developed a national known trademark in which is offering a service to all. I also hope that I would get to meet people who have been inspired through this book, who have beat obstacles through this book and have made their dream a reality through this book. I would also believe that in the next 5 years my finance would be stable. I would also this time in 5 years be thinking about investing on different projects.

What other long term plans do you have?

I hope that one day hopefully within ten years I will have developed a charity to help national and overseas young individuals believe that they have what it takes to become an entrepreneur. I would also be hoping to have invested within the UK and overseas to attract further potential business in the UK. However I believe that the opportunities are endless.

Who has inspired you?

Ive been inspired by many in the business world. I would say that the 'Dragons' on BBC 2 have inspired me. I would also say that Sir Alan Sugar has inspired me. As I can relate to his life as its very similar to mine. My biggest aspirations have been people around me.

Ive been around people who have done really well for themselves. Therefore I have thought if they can do it why cant I? Another aspiration of mine has been a student called Alex Tew.

His idea the www.milliondollarhomepage.com was an intriguing business which really caught my eye. He sold 1,000,000 pixels for one dollar therefore making him very successful. Lastly I just relish the prospects of being involved within a business environment. Its obviously the money but its also that feeling you get when you have done something with your life.

What advice would you give to anyone wanting to become an entrepreneur?

My advice to anyone who would want to become an entrepreneur would be go for it. Don't leave it for another day make something happen. Your business could be worth millions, why not see if you can make that million. Don't let anyone tell you differently. However what I would recommend is get business advice don't keep it to yourself, share it with others. Speak to your friends see if they would be willing to support you on your business idea. I would also say make sure you find the right equilibrium between business and also school work/ social life.

What I have realised is that life is too short not to be enjoyed. If you relish the prospect of becoming your own boss for it...then open a business. The problem with many is that they do want to become rich and successful, however none are prepared to go to success. Well the reality is success never comes. You have to go to it.

"A brand for a company is like a reputation for a person.
You earn reputation by trying to do hard things well"

Jeff Bezos – Founder of Amazon

Business Advice and Support in the UK

Learndirect

A wealth of information about training
and education options open to you.

www.learndirect-advice.co.uk

0800 100 900

Business Link

Support and Advice on setting up a business.

www.businesslink.gov.uk

0845 600 9 006

The Prince's Trust

Advice and support for individuals wanting
to start in business.

aged 18-30.

www.princes-trust.org.uk

0800 842 842

110

Social Enterprise Coalition

For more information on social enterprises.

www.socialenterprise.org.uk

020 7793 2323

Make Your Mark

Helps you to have ideas and make them happen

www.makeyourmark.org.uk/

020 7430 8010

National Federation of Enterprise Agencies

Find your local enterprise agency and get some help and advice.

www.nfea.com

01234 831623

They are here to help :

CONTACT OUR NETWORK:

The 'How Can I' Team are available on hand to offer you free guidance and support to making your next crucial steps to becoming 'The Ultimate Entrepreneur' using our new network.

Network through e-mail with your enquiry:

support@howcanionline.com

Activities:

```
Y  M  J  A  Z  E  K  Y  E  N  O  M  T
W  V  O  B  B  N  V  J  A  Z  S  N  C
X  A  Y  G  U  T  K  S  S  C  I  Q  O
T  M  S  P  S  R  R  U  M  A  W  J  V
G  X  I  Z  I  E  O  Q  E  V  N  H  V
N  E  H  H  N  P  Y  I  Y  F  N  A  C
I  M  R  C  E  R  W  K  P  I  O  D  G
T  A  A  R  S  E  E  T  O  N  D  V  Y
E  U  L  A  S  N  N  U  U  A  N  I  U
K  F  L  E  A  E  T  A  N  N  O  C  S
R  Q  O  S  X  U  X  T  D  C  L  E  C
A  Q  D  E  W  R  S  M  C  E  F  H  U
M  C  D  R  X  Q  Z  K  D  Z  P  U  U
```

ADVICE	MARKETING
BUSINESS	MONEY
DOLLAR	NEWYORK
ENTREPRENEUR	POUND
FINANCE	RESEARCH
LONDON	

Sudoku

	2	1	4
	1		
		3	
2	3	4	

³	2	1	4
	1	²	
¹ ₄		3	¹ ²
2	3	4	

115

Sudoku Answers

3	2	1	4
4	1	2	3
1	4	3	2
2	3	4	1

Spot the 10 **differences**:

Spotted:

1-3 : Try Again 4-5 : A Little More Practice 6-7 : Getting There 8 : Almost There 9 - 10 : You could be the next successful entrepreneur

HOW CAN I....

Dream Less,

Win more?

"Sound business advice and inspirational quotes to encourage teenagers and adults to become the ultimate entrepreneur"

www.howcanionline.com

www.ingramcontent.com/pod-product-compliance
Lightning Source LLC
Chambersburg PA
CBHW072211170526
45158CB00002BA/551